W9-DAV-810

FAMOUS FIGURES OF

WYATT EARP

THE AMERICAN FRONTIER

WYATT EARP

THE AMERICAN FRONTIER

ROB STAEGER

CHELSEA HOUSE PUBLISHERS
PHILADELPHIA

For my father, a man of courage, peace, and integrity.

Produced for Chelsea House by
OTTN Publishing, Stockton, NJ

CHELSEA HOUSE PUBLISHERS
Editor in Chief: Sally Cheney
Associate Editor in Chief: Kim Shinners
Production Manager: Pamela Loos
Art Director: Sara Davis
Series Designer: Keith Trego

First Printing

1 3 5 7 9 8 6 4 2

The Chelsea House World Wide Web address is
http://www.chelseahouse.com

Library of Congress Cataloging-in-Publication Data

Staeger, Rob.
Wyatt Earp / Rob Staeger.
    p.   cm. – (Famous figures of the American frontier)
Includes bibliographical references (p.) and index.
Summary: Relates events in the personal and professional life
of a marshal with nerves of steel, Wyatt Earp, who was known
as a peacemaker until the gunfight at the O.K. Corral.
    ISBN 0-7910-6485-9 (alk. paper)
    ISBN 0-7910-6486-7 (pbk.: alk. paper)
1. Earp, Wyatt, 1848-1929--Juvenile literature. 2. Peace offi-
cers--Southwest, New--Biography--Juvenile literature. 3.
United States marshals--Southwest, New--Biography--Juvenile
literature. 4. Southwest, New--Biography--Juvenile literature.
5. Tombstone (Ariz.)--History--Juvenile literature. [1. Earp,
Wyatt, 1848-1929. 2. Peace officers. 3. Tombstone (Ariz.)--
History.]   I. Title. II. Series.

F786.E18 S73 2001
978'.02'092--dc21   2001028867

CONTENTS

The O.K. Corral

The gunfight at the O.K. Corral is probably the most famous shoot-out of the Old West. When the smoke cleared after 30 violent seconds, three men were dead, and Wyatt Earp and his friends had asserted their control over Tombstone, Arizona.

Eight men faced each other from two sides of a vacant lot. On one side were the Earp brothers, Tombstone's lawmen. They had come with their friend Doc Holliday to disarm a group of cowboys. (At the time, the term *cowboy* wasn't used as it is today. It was a name for horse thieves and cattle **rustlers**.)

Ike Clanton was the unofficial leader of this gang of

cowboys. As Ike faced the Earp brothers, he stood with his own brother Billy as well as the McLaury brothers, Frank and Tom. They had no intention of being disarmed.

Wyatt Earp had sized up the cowboys. He knew that Frank McLaury was the best shot of the bunch. But when Wyatt made his move, no one could tell if he drew his gun first, or if Billy Clanton had; their two shots sounded almost at once. Billy fired at Wyatt, missing him, while Wyatt shot Frank McLaury in the stomach. Wyatt's brother Virgil drew his pistol from the waistband of his pants, and the younger Morgan Earp fired his pistol. Wyatt's best friend, Doc Holliday, aimed Virgil's shotgun, which had been hidden in his long coat. In a moment, everyone was fighting.

Frank McLaury may have been a great shot under normal circumstances, but now, with a bullet in his gut, he was not doing so well. His brother Tom crouched behind Frank's horse, firing a rifle. Doc Holliday blazed back at Tom with his own shotgun. Morgan Earp had hit Billy Clanton twice, once in the right wrist and once in the chest. As Billy slumped against the wall of a nearby house, he switched his pistol to his left hand and tried to fire.

Ike Clanton didn't seem to be armed. He ran up to Wyatt and grabbed his arm, begging for his life. Wyatt pushed him aside. "The fight has commenced," he said. "Go to fighting, or get away." Clanton, always more wily than brave, ran away as his friends and brother were dying.

Bullets flew for 30 seconds. At the end of the gunfight, three of the cowboys—Billy Clanton and Tom and Frank McLaury—were dead. As for the Earps, Virgil was shot in the calf, and a bullet had grazed Morgan's shoulder blades. Doc was wounded in the hip. Only Wyatt walked away unscathed.

What had led Wyatt Earp to this gunfight? Until now, he had always been known for his restraint in dealing with criminals. The shoot-out, however, made him famous for a spectacular moment of violence. It became known as "the gunfight at the O.K. Corral." From this point on, Wyatt's name would call up images of a lawman gone over the edge. And a fight that began in the vacant lot near Fly's Photography Studio would end months later as a ground war waged across Arizona.

Over the years Wyatt Earp has been given the reputation of a lawman who shot first and asked questions later. Although Earp was not afraid of fights, he did not look for trouble; he preferred to solve problems without violence when possible.

EARLY DAYS

Wyatt Berry Stapp Earp was born in Monmouth, Illinois, on March 19, 1848, the son of Nicholas and Virginia Ann Earp. Wyatt had three older brothers: Newton, James, and Virgil.

When Wyatt was two, the Earps left Monmouth to farm in Pella, Iowa. This was the first of many moves for Wyatt, since Nicholas and Virginia didn't stay in one

Nicholas Earp had served under Captain Wyatt Berry Stapp during the Mexican-American War. He named his son after his former commander, a man he respected.

place for long. In Iowa, Wyatt's younger brothers Morgan and Warren were born. They were followed by his sisters Virginia, Adelia, and Martha. Of the Earp sisters, only Adelia survived childhood.

Wyatt was 13 when the Civil War began in 1861. His older brothers all **enlisted** in the Union Army. Wyatt was determined to do the same, but his father stopped him from joining the army.

Wyatt had to wait three years before he saw the action he craved. His chance came during his family's journey to San Bernardino, California. When the Earp family joined a westbound **wagon train**, Wyatt helped defend the wagon train from Indian attacks.

In California, Virgil got a job driving a stagecoach, and Wyatt was paid to ride along. By 1868, however, the Earps were on the move again. They eventually settled in Lamar, Missouri.

In January of 1870, Wyatt married Urilla Sutherland, the daughter of a hotel owner. Urilla died that summer, possibly due to **typhoid** complications during childbirth. Soon after her death, the Earps met Urilla's brothers in a street fight. The Sutherland brothers believed Urilla had been too young to marry and blamed Wyatt for her death.

Soon afterward, Wyatt was elected *constable* of Lamar, his first job in law enforcement. He beat his brother Newton in the election by 35 votes.

In March of 1871, Wyatt was accused of misusing his position as constable. A man named James Cromwell said Wyatt had over-charged him for an

> Wyatt and Newton may have run against each other simply to make sure the constable job went to an Earp. Whatever the reason, neither had any hard feelings about the election. Years later, Newt even named his son after Wyatt.

official service. Cromwell accused him of stealing the extra money. But by the time Cromwell made his accusation, Wyatt had already left Lamar. Did he leave because he knew trouble was coming? Or did Cromwell only feel comfortable accusing the tough Earp after he was gone?

Either way, Wyatt's troubles with the law weren't over yet. A few weeks later, Wyatt and two other men, Edward Kennedy and John Shown, were accused of stealing horses. In the West, horse theft was treated almost as harshly as murder. The three were arrested. However, *testimony* from Shown's wife got the charges against him dropped. Kennedy was tried first and found not guilty. After that defeat, prosecutors lost interest in the case. Wyatt's case never even made it to trial.

Wyatt spent the next two years wandering the West. He took a job as a *surveyor* and later worked as a buffalo hunter. While hunting buffalo, Wyatt befriended Bartholomew "Bat" Masterson.

Wyatt's reputation as a fearless, no-nonsense lawman began in Ellsworth, Kansas. Ironically, no one is certain that he actually was an officer of the law at the time. The incident started when a thug named Billy Thompson got drunk and gunned down Ellsworth's sheriff. To cover his retreat, Billy's brother Ben and some friends held the town at gunpoint. None of the police was willing to face Ben's gang. Legend says that Ellsworth's mayor made Wyatt a deputy *marshal* on the spot.

Wyatt walked right up to Ben Thompson and told him to lay down his guns. Amazingly, Thompson did. Wyatt freed the town without firing a shot. This earned him a reputation as a peacemaker with nerves of steel.

Thompson was fined only $25 for holding up the town. Hearing this, Wyatt is said to have returned his badge, complaining about the low value Ellsworth put on its deputies.

In 1874 Wyatt moved to Wichita, Kansas, where he joined the police force. The Wichita newspapers loved Wyatt, praising him equally for his honesty and his reluctance to kill. One famous incident relates Wyatt jailing a drunk who had a $500 bankroll. Many a western lawman might have pocketed some or all of the money, but Wyatt released the man the next day with every dollar still in his pocket. The *Wichita Beacon* said of the released man, "He may congratulate himself that his lines, while he was drunk, were cast in such a pleasant place as Wichita as there are but few other places where that $500 roll would ever [have] been heard from."

Wyatt's integrity may have been what led him into a petty disagreement with his boss, Marshal Bill Smith. Unfortunately, his temper was what escalated the argument into a fistfight. Smith fired Wyatt, and Wyatt left town not long after. He soon found himself in Dodge City, the roughest, meanest town in the West.

Wyatt Earp is seated in the front, second from the left, in this photo of Dodge City lawmen. His good friend Bat Masterson is standing at the right; next to him is another friend of the Earps, Luke Short. While Earp and Masterson were lawmen in Dodge during the late 1870s, they stashed shotguns in hiding places throughout the town, so they would be close at hand in an emergency.

DODGE CITY

People in Kansas claim that the phrase "the wrong side of the tracks" began in Dodge City. The cattle town, located near the Arkansas River, was a dangerous place. Daylight muggings and nighttime shootings were common. As for the tracks, they ran along Front Street, through the center of town. North of Front Street were a market, a dry goods shop, and other stores. South were saloons, casinos, **brothels**, and dance halls. These establishments kept the visiting cowhands entertained during **cattle drives**. But drunk, rowdy cowhands are bound to cause trouble. In the lawless atmosphere of Dodge City, they often did.

When Wyatt Earp arrived in May of 1876, his brother Morgan was already working there as deputy. Mayor George Hoover immediately hired Wyatt to be assistant city marshal under Marshal Larry Deger. The job of marshal was mostly deskbound, which suited the 300-pound Deger. That left Wyatt to be the city's chief lawman in the streets of Dodge.

Wyatt made the dangerous town considerably safer. He hired Bat Masterson to help him. Together, they turned Dodge into a place where crime was, if not eliminated, at least controlled. And they accomplished this without much shooting. Earp told his biographer, Stuart Lake, "Hoover had hired me to cut down the killings in Dodge, not increase them."

Often, to corral a troublemaker, Wyatt would walk up behind him. Then he'd knock him on the head with his gun barrel. Earp and Masterson called the technique "buffaloing," since they had learned it years before while hunting buffalo. The name stuck.

Frederic Remington drew this illustration of a gunfight between two men outside a saloon. Actually, gunfights in Dodge and other Kansas "cow towns" were relatively rare. From 1870 to 1885, a total of 45 murders were committed in the five largest cattle towns—Dodge, Wichita, Abilene, Caldwell, and Ellsworth—an average of less than one per year in each town.

In cattle towns, trouble came mostly during the cattle drives. So, most police jobs were seasonal. Wyatt found winter work with Wells Fargo, a freight and banking company. He guarded gold shipments as they traveled through the region. (The guard's position, holding a weapon while seated next to the stagecoach driver, gave rise to the phrase "riding shotgun.") At other times, Wyatt and Morgan spent their time looking for gold in the Black Hills.

Wyatt never let politics get in the way of the law. Shortly after arriving in Dodge, Wyatt arrested cattleman Bob Rachal. Rachal had been shooting at a musician on Front Street. Bob Wright, one of Dodge's founders, tried to use his political clout to protest the arrest. Wyatt wouldn't hear of it, though. He put Wright in his place, and kept Rachal in jail.

In 1877, though, when spring came, Wyatt did not officially rejoin the police force. Instead, he spent the year on the gambling circuit. He may have worked as an undercover **bounty hunter** for Wells Fargo.

While Wyatt was gone, Dodge became more violent. In April 1878, Sheriff Ed Masterson, Bat's brother, was killed trying to disarm a cowboy. He was shot in the chest at such close range that his shirt caught on fire. Wyatt was immediately rehired as assistant marshal.

Soon after this, Wyatt met the man who would become his best friend. On June 8, 1878, John "Doc" Holliday first advertised his dental practice in the *Dodge City Times*. He had a reputation as a dangerous and violent man. People said he had killed several men, but no one had ever seen him do it. Perhaps Holliday built the reputation himself.

Wyatt claimed his friendship with Holliday

began when Doc saved his life. No one knows for sure how this happened. In Wyatt's biography, *Frontier Marshal,* Stuart Lake writes that Doc stood off 50 rowdy cowboys who were threatening Wyatt. In an 1896 newspaper interview, Wyatt told a different story. He said that Doc shot a man who was aiming at Wyatt's back. This is more believable, but Dodge City has no records to prove either story. Possibly, Doc simply shouted a warning when Wyatt needed one. That doesn't make an exciting newspaper story, but it could certainly spark a friendship. In any case, Doc was a constant, loyal friend to Wyatt. Despite his reputation, Doc never killed anyone in Dodge City. When Wyatt was around, Doc stayed close to the straight and narrow.

Also around the same time he met Doc, Wyatt began seeing a woman named Celia Ann "Mattie" Blaylock. Mattie's early history is a blank, since historians have not found any record of her before she left Dodge with Wyatt. There's no official marriage record, but she was probably his ***common-law wife***.

On the night of July 25, 1878, the Earps and their friends were on the south side of the tracks—the wrong side—listening to a musician. Suddenly, three men started shooting outside. Bullets punched through the walls of the music hall. Bat Masterson and Doc Holliday threw themselves to the floor. Bat's brother Jim and Wyatt fired back, and the gunmen rode away. One of them, George Hoy, was shot in the back by Wyatt. Hoy died a month later. He was the first man Wyatt ever killed.

The incident troubled Wyatt. He began to believe Bob Rachal or Bob Wright, powerful men in Dodge whom he had angered, were plotting to kill him. However, no one has ever proved that a plot did in fact exist. Wyatt, feeling guilty for killing Hoy, may have simply seized on the idea as a way to justify his own actions to himself.

Clay Allison, however, soon came to town, and he was looking for Wyatt. Allison was a murderous *hired gun* who often worked for Rachal and White. When Wyatt confronted Allison on the street, Allison accused him of killing Hoy. Wyatt admitted this, but he also let Allison know that at that moment Bat Masterson had a shotgun aimed at him from a nearby window. Wyatt had his right hand on his holstered gun. His left hand was ready to grab Allison's weapon if he drew it. Allison never drew. He realized the odds were against him and backed off. Wyatt's reputation as a fierce lawman increased without his firing a shot.

The last big case Wyatt would confront in Dodge was a high-profile murder. James "Spike" Kenedy had a grudge against Dodge's mayor, Jim Kelley. In October 1878, he rode up to Kelley's house and fired his gun into it four times. He didn't realize that Kelley was at a hospital in Fort Dodge. The popular actress Dora Hand was staying in his house while he was away. One shot killed Hand.

Wyatt joined Bat Masterson's posse to track Kenedy down. After two days, they saw Kenedy approaching them. Three times, they told him to surrender, but instead, Kenedy reached for his gun and fired. Bat and Wyatt shot back. Bat knocked Kenedy down with a bullet in the shoulder. Wyatt shot his horse. "I hated to do it," Wyatt later said. "Kenedy's horse was a beauty." Nonetheless, they took Kenedy in without killing him.

Not long afterward, Wyatt began to feel that Dodge was "losing its snap." The once-lawless town had been tamed. He resigned on September 9, 1879, and headed west.

TOMBSTONE

This picture of downtown Tombstone, Arizona, was taken in 1880, around the time Wyatt Earp arrived in town. On the right the sign for the Oriental Saloon, one of Wyatt's favorite hangouts, is visible. The town had only been established in early 1879; two years later the population had grown to 5,600.

After they left Dodge, Wyatt and Mattie visited Virgil in Prescott, Arizona. When they arrived, Virgil had just been offered a deputy marshal job in Tombstone, Arizona. Tombstone was a booming new town founded after a *silver strike* there the year before. People had flocked to the area to stake their own *claims*, and Wyatt thought it would be a good place to establish a stagecoach line. Virgil accepted the deputy job, and Wyatt and Mattie moved with him to Tombstone. Doc Holliday followed soon after.

When the brothers arrived in November, Wyatt's hopes for setting up a stagecoach business were dashed. The town already had two good stage lines, so Wyatt had to find other work. He staked two mining claims, but neither yielded any silver. Then a businessman named Lou Rickabaugh approached him with a problem. A bully named Johnny Tyler was driving patrons away from Rickabaugh's gambling tables at the Oriental Saloon. Rickabaugh offered Wyatt part of the business profit if he would keep Tyler away. Wyatt intimidated Tyler, who left immediately. Wyatt began to deal cards at the Oriental, keeping his eye out for trouble.

Wyatt's favorite handgun was this ivory-handled, nickel-plated 1873 Colt .45. This model, nicknamed the "Peacemaker," was one of the most popular weapons among lawmen and gunfighters in the West. Wyatt's gun was single-action, meaning that the hammer had to be manually cocked before it would fire.

Wyatt didn't become a police officer in Tombstone until the summer of 1880. On July 21, six mules were stolen from nearby Fort Rucker. Curly Bill Brocius, a local cowboy, was suspected. Virgil traced the mules and Curly Bill to the McLaury ranch. He hired Wyatt and Morgan as special officers for the case. When the Earps rode to the ranch with Lieutenant Hurst from Fort Rucker, they found men trying to change the army **brand** of "US" into "D8." Trying to keep peace, Hurst struck a deal with Frank McLaury instead of arresting him. The arrangement did not work out, however, and Hurst called for McLaury's arrest in a local newspaper, the *Tombstone Epitaph*.

When McLaury read the newspaper, he burst into Virgil's office, offended that his good name had been smeared. Wyatt was astonished at McLaury's arrogance. He signed on as a permanent deputy.

A few months later, Curly Bill caused trouble again—this time fatal trouble. He and some other cowboys started shooting out the Tombstone street-lamps. City marshal Fred White, a friend of the Earps, approached Bill to disarm him. Bill's pistol went off as he handed it to White, killing the marshal. Wyatt immediately "buffaloed" Bill and took him to jail. However, White's last words kept Bill from being convicted. The dying man insisted the shooting was an accident. Virgil was appointed city marshal in White's place.

Around this time, Arizona's counties were being restructured. Wyatt applied for appointment as sheriff of Tombstone's new county, Cochise County. A low-level politician named John Behan also wanted the job, so he made a deal with Wyatt. If Wyatt wouldn't take the job, Behan would make Wyatt undersheriff. In truth, the active job of under-sheriff was better suited to Wyatt's hands-on style of peacekeeping. He accepted, but Behan went back on his word. He hired Harry Woods, editor of the *Daily Nugget,* instead. Wyatt and Behan were unfriendly from then on.

Fueling the feud was Josephine Marcus, an actress who had met Behan in Prescott, Arizona. Josie (also known sometimes as Sadie) moved in with Behan and took care of his 10-year-old son Albert. The relationship between Behan and Josie was stormy and at times physically abusive. After finding Behan with another woman, Josie left him and found an apartment in town. Soon she caught Wyatt's attention. Despite his common-law

Virgil Earp was appointed marshal of Tombstone after his friend Fred White was accidentally killed by a cowboy.

marriage with Mattie, Wyatt struck up a friendship with Josie. The friendship grew into a romance, as Wyatt began taking Josie to Tombstone's fancier restaurants. Seeing this courtship, Behan drew the obvious conclusion—Wyatt had stolen his girlfriend. If Wyatt had had just cause to resent Behan before, now Behan had as good a reason to resent Wyatt.

In January of 1881, Wyatt saved the life of Mike Rourke, a gambler nicknamed "Johnny Behind-the-Deuce." Rourke, who had killed a man, was being taken to another prison in Tucson when a mob surrounded him, ready to *lynch* him. Wyatt stepped between Rourke and the crowd. He held them off, laying his life on the line for a criminal's safety.

Around this time, Wyatt's prize racehorse, Dick Naylor, was stolen. Hearing that it was in Charleston, Wyatt and Doc Holliday rode to that town. They found the horse in a corral, with 18-year-old cowboy Billy Clanton nearby. Though he gave the horse back, Clanton said he'd steal it again if he could. Understandably, the dislike between the cowboys and the Earps grew.

The cowboys were obviously cattle thieves, but some of the people of Tombstone still stood behind them. They did so for several reasons. First, most of the stolen cattle belonged to Mexican ranchers, and many people in Tombstone didn't like Mexicans. They didn't care if Mexicans' property was stolen. Second, the thieves weren't the only ones making money off the stolen cattle. From butchers to other ranchers, many people in Tombstone profited from the thefts. These people didn't consider themselves dishonest, even though they were dealing with thieves. Still, they knew they owed their good fortune to bad deeds. And last, siding with the cowboys was a matter of class and politics. The Civil War had ended only 15 years before, and feelings were still strong on both sides. Friends of the cowboys were Democrats, mostly ranchers and farmhands who had supported the South in the Civil War. Friends of the Earps were mostly Republicans, northern businessmen and gamblers who had supported the Union. Reducing the situation to country folk versus city folk may be too simple, but those tensions certainly played a part.

Public opinion was always divided about the Earps. Some people admired the way they kept the peace. Others felt they were too zealous in their pursuit of the law, trampling over people's rights. The two newspapers in town reflected these views. The *Tombstone Epitaph* backed the Earps. The *Nugget*, run by Behan's undersheriff, Harry Woods, sided with the cowboys.

On March 15, 1881, several men tried to hold up a stagecoach on its 30-mile trek from Tombstone to Benson, Arizona. It was carrying a Wells Fargo shipment of $26,000. The thieves opened fire, killing two men, but the stage escaped to Benson.

Virgil Earp organized a *posse* to catch the bandits. Wyatt and Morgan rode with him, and soon they were joined by other lawmen, including Sheriff Behan. Riding ahead of the posse, Wyatt and Morgan caught and questioned a suspect named Luther King. Behan took King back to the

Tombstone jail. The Earp posse rode for a few more days but found nothing.

When the posse rode back to Tombstone, they got some bad news. Sheriff Behan had let Luther King escape. Worse, Doc Holliday was arrested for being one of the bandits. His girlfriend, Kate Elder, had told the police that Holliday was involved in the attempted robbery. Doc and Kate had been arguing, and this was her revenge. Eventually, Kate admitted she had made the story up, and Doc was released.

In mid-April, two Earp friends, Bat Masterson and Luke Short, left Tombstone. This left the Earps vulnerable in a time when the cowboys were getting stronger and more daring.

To make matters worse, Tombstone suffered a horrible fire that June. Wyatt rescued a woman from the second floor of a burning building, but over 60 buildings were destroyed in the blaze. Soon, **lot jumpers** set up camp in the cinders. The Earps had their hands full driving them away.

On September 8, two masked men robbed the Bisbee stagecoach. One of the bandits was heard calling the money "sugar," a slang term Frank Stilwell was known to use. Based on that evidence, Wyatt arrested Stilwell, who was John Behan's

John Behan, the sheriff of Cochise County, was Wyatt's rival—both for the job of sheriff and for the attention of a young woman named Josephine Marcus. Sheriff Behan represented the law in the countryside, while the Earps were responsible for keeping the peace in Tombstone.

deputy sheriff, and his partner, Pete Spence. They were soon released on bail, however.

Because mail had been on the stagecoach, and interference with mail delivery was a federal crime, Virgil arrested them once more—but again they were released. Some frustrated citizens wanted to take the law into their own hands. Virgil worried that the townspeople might become a mob. To help him keep the peace, he appointed Morgan as a special officer on October 12.

But peace wouldn't come soon to Tombstone. The most famous shoot-out of the West was two weeks away.

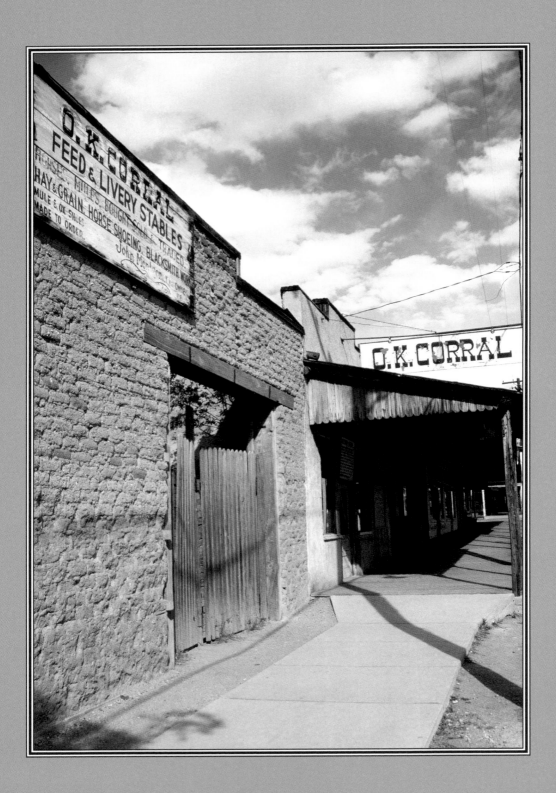

The gunfight at the O.K. Corral actually took place about a half-block away, in a vacant lot about 20 feet wide between two houses. By waiting there for the showdown with the Earps, the Clantons and McLaurys had boxed themselves in. There was no room for them to move, and no place to hide.

30 Seconds

While questioning Luther King, Wyatt had learned the names of three other robbers. Wells Fargo offered a $6,000 reward for their capture. Wyatt wanted to be sheriff more than he wanted the money. He rode out to Ike Clanton's ranch and offered him the reward if he would get Wyatt the robbers. The glory of capturing these thieves would make Wyatt a shoo-in for sheriff.

Ike accepted the deal, but he asked Wyatt to keep it secret. He didn't want his other cowboy friends to find out he was planning to help the other side. Soon afterward, the Wells Fargo agent told Clanton that he knew about the deal. Clanton stormed into Wyatt's office and accused Wyatt of telling Doc Holliday about their bargain. Maybe Clanton thought the agent had heard about the deal from Holliday. In any case, Holliday got angry and told Clanton he didn't know anything about it.

Holliday and Clanton argued again the night of October 25, but Morgan and Wyatt stopped them from fighting. At one o'clock in the morning, drunk but still making threats, Clanton left the Earps and Holliday. He did not go home, though. Instead, he went to the Occidental Saloon, where he played poker until 6 A.M. Shortly after the game, Clanton apparently started drinking again. He threatened to kill Doc Holliday and wandered the streets of Tombstone, waving a gun around. By dawn, most of the town knew trouble was coming.

People warned Virgil and Wyatt about Clanton's threats. Virgil and Morgan found him in the streets, and Virgil crept up behind him and took his gun. He took Clanton to court for carrying a weapon, because carrying a gun in town was illegal if you weren't a police officer. He was fined $25.

Outside the court, Wyatt spoke with Tom McLaury, but no one knows what was said. Did McLaury threaten the Earps? Or did Wyatt misinterpret his words? Either way, the conversation ended in blows, and Wyatt beat McLaury to the ground. If McLaury didn't have a grudge against the Earps before, he did now.

At two o'clock, Ike and Billy Clanton and Tom and Frank McLaury gathered at Spangenberg's gun shop. From there, they walked to a vacant lot on Fremont Street, around the corner from the O.K.

After threatening Doc Holliday on the night of October 25, Ike Clanton played poker with Tom McLaury, John Behan, Virgil Earp, and an unknown player. The game broke up at 6 A.M. No one knows what went on during this game, but in a few hours, these men would be standing in a vacant lot, trying to kill each other.

38 WYATT EARP

Corral. Sheriff Behan was afraid of a brawl between the townspeople and the cowboys. He approached the gang. The Clantons and McLaurys refused to give up their weapons unless the Earps were disarmed first.

At 2:30, Doc Holliday met the Earps at Hafford's Corner Saloon. He insisted on going with them to meet the gang. Hoping to avoid trouble, Virgil traded his shotgun for Doc's cane, so that Virgil could appear unarmed. Doc hid Virgil's shotgun under his long coat. Virgil still had his pistol, but he didn't think that would provoke a fight.

Behan met the Earps on Fremont Street. They understood him to say that he'd already disarmed the cowboys. Either Behan was lying, or the Earps

John Holliday, nicknamed "Doc" because of his dental practice, was suffering from tuberculosis when he arrived in Tombstone.

heard him wrong. As the Earps continued on their way, they could see the cowboys waiting for them, their hands on their guns.

The guns startled Virgil, but Wyatt was ready. The gunfire lasted for 30 seconds. By the time it stopped, Doc, Virgil, and Morgan were wounded. Billy Clanton and the McLaurys were dead.

After the shoot-out, Sheriff Behan tried to arrest Wyatt, but Wyatt refused to surrender to him. Instead, he tended his wounded brothers and friend. The next day, both the *Epitaph* and the *Nugget* printed stories favorable to the Earps. The *Nugget's* story was unusual, since Harry Woods's paper usually backed the cowboys.

Soon, Ike Clanton filed murder charges against the Earps and Holliday, and a formal trial began. Justice Wells Spicer set bail at $10,000 apiece for Doc and the Earps. They raised the money quickly; what Wyatt's business holdings in Tombstone could not cover was offset by money from Wells Fargo and local miners. The law-abiding people of Tombstone didn't want to see the Earps in jail.

Meanwhile, Tombstone was getting dangerous for the Earps. On October 31, James Earp went to Virgil's house. He found a man disguised as a

Victims of the gunfight at the O.K. Corral: Frank McLaury (left), shot by both Wyatt and Morgan Earp; Tom McLaury (center), fatally wounded by a blast from Doc Holliday's shotgun; and Billy Clanton (right), the youngest of the group, who was still trying to fire his pistol as he lay dying on the sidewalk after the shoot-out.

woman lurking there. The Earps believed that the man had been sent to kill Virgil, Wyatt, or Morgan. The Earp women (Virgil's wife Allie, Morgan's wife Louisa, and Wyatt's common-law wife Mattie) moved immediately to the Cosmopolitan Hotel, where security would be better. The wounded Morgan and Virgil soon joined them there.

The trial began with Sheriff Behan's testimony. He claimed that Tom McLaury was unarmed when the fight began, and that Doc Holliday had shot first with his "nickel-plated pistol." Behan was very specific about Doc's nickel-plated pistol, a gun for which Holliday was well known. Doc would have been unlikely to use the pistol to fire first, since he was holding Virgil's shotgun at the time.

The prosecution was joined by Tom and Frank's brother, Will McLaury, a lawyer from Fort Worth, Texas. He believed his brothers were innocent and came to defend the family honor. The young lawyer arrived just in time to see Ike Clanton start to blow the case apart.

Ike's testimony was unbelievable. First, he claimed that he'd never threatened the Earps. Then he said the Earps were responsible for the recent stagecoach robberies and that Doc Holliday had shot a stage driver through the heart. According to Ike, the gunfight had been started by the Earps specifically to kill him, since he knew too much about their criminal activities.

Ike's story fell apart when he was questioned by the Earps' defense. For one thing, if the purpose of the gunfight was to kill him, why wasn't he dead? Wyatt and the others certainly had plenty of chances to shoot him. Also, Ike had no proof that the Earps robbed the stagecoaches; he just claimed that they had told him so. But why would these men tell their enemy, Ike Clanton, secrets they told no one else? Obviously, Ike was lying.

The defense began its case with a prepared statement by Wyatt Earp. Wyatt's statement listed all his troubles with the cowboys, including the killing of Marshal White and Billy Clanton's theft of Wyatt's horse. Then he explained the bargain he had made with Ike for the Benson stage robbers. He followed that with his version of the gunfight, which matched the newspaper reports. Finally, to answer any statements against his character, Wyatt presented a petition. It was signed by 62 prominent Kansas citizens of Wichita and Dodge City. Some of them, such as Bob Wright, had even argued with Wyatt in the past, but on the issue of his integrity, they agreed. The petition read, "We do not believe that he would wantonly take the life of his fellow man."

Virgil testified next. He confirmed Wyatt's story about the gunfight and insisted that the cowboys were armed. But the testimony that turned the tide was that of H. F. Sills, a railroad engineer. Sills, who had witnessed the fight, backed Wyatt's version. He was also the first witness to mention Ike's threats to the Earps the night before. Once Ike's threats were on record, other witnesses confirmed them. Also, Addie Bourland, a dressmaker who lived across from Fly's studio, saw the entire gunfight. She did not see Doc fire first. She said that the cowboys did not have their hands up when the shots began.

As always, public opinion was not entirely behind the Earps. After the shooting, the bodies of Billy Clanton and the McLaurys were propped up at Ritter and Ream, City Undertakers. Over them, a sign read, "Murdered in the Streets of Tombstone"—the same inscription that appears on this grave marker.

Justice Spicer stated that at first glance, Virgil's decision to get his brothers' help in approaching the cowboys did not seem wise. However, it turned out that he needed "staunch and true friends, upon whose courage, coolness, and fidelity he could depend, in case of an emergency." The gunfight was certainly an emergency, and Virgil could not have survived it alone. The judge found the Earps and Holliday not guilty.

Wyatt and Doc were released on December 1. One of the first things Wyatt did was register to vote in Cochise County. This sent a signal to the cowboys: Wyatt Earp was in Tombstone to stay.

The cowboys would do their best to change that.

The violence in Tombstone did not end with the gunfight at the O.K. Corral. After Virgil Earp was badly injured in one attack and Morgan Earp killed in another, Wyatt went after his enemies. However, he decided to step outside of the law, killing the men he believed responsible rather than arresting them and bringing them to trial.

VENDETTA RIDE

By the end of 1881, Virgil Earp, like most of his family, was living in the Cosmopolitan Hotel. On December 28, he was ambushed on his way home. Two bullets struck him—one in the arm and one in the small of his back.

Because it looked like Virgil would die, Wyatt sent a telegram to the U.S. marshal, who told him to appoint deputies of his own and investigate. In the end, doctors saved Virgil's life by removing five inches of shattered bone from his arm. Though he lived, Virgil's arm was crippled by the shots.

Almost immediately, a string of robberies began. On January 6, $6,500 was stolen from the Bisbee stagecoach. The next day, the Benson stage was held up. Wyatt, Morgan, and a few other deputies armed themselves and headed out. They had arrest warrants for three cowboys: Ike Clanton, Fin Clanton, and Pony Deal. Eventually, the Clantons surrendered to federal authorities and were returned to Tombstone.

The Clantons thought they were surrendering to a charge of mail theft. Instead, they were charged with the attempted murder of Virgil Earp. Ike Clanton's hat had been found near the shooting.

The Clantons went to trial. They were found not guilty of shooting Virgil. Despite the evidence of Ike's hat, they had too many friends testifying. Each one provided an *alibi*, saying Ike was somewhere else when it happened. Both Wyatt and Judge William Stilwell felt the law had failed them. Wyatt later remembered Stilwell telling him, "Wyatt, you'll never clean up this crowd this way; next time you'd better leave your prisoners out in the brush where alibis don't count." If these words didn't inspire what followed, they did at least foretell what lay ahead.

On March 18, Morgan and Wyatt were playing pool. Suddenly the saloon door opened and two shots were fired. One bullet took a chunk out of the wall above Wyatt's head. The other tore into Morgan's back. Morgan lived for an hour. His last words were to Wyatt: "Do you know who did it?"

"Yes, and I'll get them," said Wyatt.

"That's all I'll ask. But Wyatt, be careful." And with that, Morgan died.

The next day, the Earps and Doc Holliday put Morgan's body on a train to Tucson. It would travel from there to the family home in Colton, California, where Morgan would be buried. Virgil and Allie accompanied the body, but Wyatt heard rumors of an ambush in Tucson. Wyatt knew that in Virgil's condition, he couldn't defend anyone, so Wyatt and a group of friends guarded Virgil and Allie on the train.

When the train pulled into Tucson that night, Wyatt checked the station platform. He saw Frank Stilwell and another man waiting for them on a *flat-*

car. Giving chase across the railroad tracks, Wyatt caught up with Stilwell. Stilwell pleaded for his life, but Wyatt shot him with both barrels of his shotgun. He would not let his brother's murderer get away. By shooting the man down, however, Wyatt became an outlaw.

The company he was keeping didn't help Wyatt's reputation. The only upstanding citizen in the bunch was his brother Warren. The rest included Doc Holliday, a long-haired crack shot named Texas Jack Vermillion, and two men most people thought were ordinary criminals. No one knew that Sherman McMasters and Jack Johnson were actually police informers.

Wyatt and his posse rode into Tombstone for a few hours. On their way out, Sheriff Behan tried to arrest Wyatt. Behan didn't even get the words out before Wyatt told him they would see Tucson's sheriff instead. If Wyatt were going to be arrested, he wanted a man of honor to do the deed.

Wyatt owned this double-barreled Syracuse Arms shotgun; he may have used this gun, or another like it, during his Vendetta Ride in 1881–82.

Instead, Wyatt continued to hunt for his brother's killers. When he heard Pete Spence had been involved, he rode to Spence's camp in the Dragoon Mountains. Spence was gone, though; he had surrendered himself to Sheriff Behan for protection. But the Earps were directed toward Florentino Cruz, who was nicknamed "Indian Charlie." Cruz had been the lookout when Morgan was shot, Wyatt was told.

Cornered, Cruz named the killers, including Frank Stilwell, Curly Bill Brocius, and himself. Spence had nothing to do with the murder, he said, and Wyatt believed him. Cruz's body was later found. He'd been shot four times.

All around the country, people were talking about the fighting in Arizona. Newspapers called it the *Vendetta* Ride. The nation was divided on whether Wyatt's actions were justice or revenge.

Soon Wyatt and his posse rode into Iron Springs. As they watered their horses, cowboys shot at them from the bushes. Texas Jack's horse was shot, and he was pinned under it. The rest of the posse fled for cover, but Wyatt stood his ground. Bullets whizzed around him, tearing his coat to pieces. Seeing Curly Bill in the group, Wyatt aimed and fired his shotgun. Both blasts struck Bill in the chest, killing him. Still mounted, Wyatt reached for his pistol, but he had been wearing his gun belt loose. His guns had slipped around behind him, beyond his reach. He tried to grab his rifle from the saddle behind him, but because his gun belt was loose, he couldn't turn on the horse properly. Finally, he righted himself. He pulled Texas Jack out from under his horse and left the scene. As he rode off, Wyatt felt a bullet, and his foot went numb.

When he was sure they were safe, Wyatt took his boot off. Incredibly, the bullet hadn't hit his foot but had simply lodged in his boot heel. His long coat was shredded and his shoe was damaged, but once again, not a single bullet had hit Wyatt.

Meanwhile, Sheriff Behan searched for Wyatt with a new posse. It included several cowboys, such as Pony Deal, Ike Clanton, and John Ringo. They tracked Wyatt's group to the Sierra Bonita Ranch. There, Behan was told that the Earps had left. Behan guessed they were probably on a nearby bluff, but he didn't pursue them. Finding them would have risked his life. He returned to Tombstone empty-handed.

More battles may have been fought during the

Vendetta Ride, but nothing is known about them. If he killed anyone else, Wyatt covered his tracks more carefully. By mid-April, the ride was over. The Earps had left Tombstone, and Wyatt would never return. But Tombstone would stay with Wyatt for the rest of his life.

THE WHITE PASS CHRONICLE

GROWING WITH THE LAST GREAT FRONTIER

NEWS FROM THE KLONDIKE.

GOLD! GOLD! GOLD! GOLD!

Special Tug Chartered To Get The News.

The Land Of Gold

dream dreams.
way sheer walls
2, 1898, it ran

sion of man's
timeless march

onomic depres-
entific advance-

haps within the
bile will zoom
eds. Man may
take to the air
of nations will
who are still to
common cold,
way sound, frail
d his footprints

gons Running
Dawson Soon

WHITE HORSE TODAY

BUILDING BOOMING

White Horse, Apr. 1, 1901 — The spring boom has struck White Horse in earnest. The sound of hammers can be heard in all directions and vacant lots in the business portion of the town are becoming as scarce as mushrooms on an iceberg.

Many substantial frame buildings are going up, also many canvas ones which in time will give place to more permanent structures.

About 400 men are at present working in the town with the prospect of many more being employed, and in the evening the streets put one in mind of the great thoroughfares of the large cities throughout the states.

SKAGWAY AND UP RIVER POINTS

Alex Schwartz and Party Leave Bennett By Boat

Seattle, July 17, 1897. ON BOARD THE STEAMSHIP PORTLAND, 3:00 A.M. — At 3 o'clock this morning the steamship Portland, from St. Michaels for Seattle, passed up the Sound with more than a ton of solid gold on board and 68 passengers. In the captain's cabin are three chests and a large safe filled with the precious nuggets. The metal is worth nearly $700,000 and most of it was taken from the Klondike district in less than three months last winter. In size the nuggets range from the size of a pea to a guinea hen egg. Of the 68 miners on board hardly a man has less than $7,000, and one or two have more than $100,000 in yellow nuggets.

QUEEN VICTORIA

Clarence Berry is regarded as the luckiest man in the Klondike. Ten months ago he was a poor miner and to-day he is in Seattle with $130,000 in gold nuggets. One nugget weighs 13 ounces and is worth $231. "I've been rather fortunate," he averred.

Inspector Strickland, of the North West Mounted Police, was guarded with his statements. He said there were only two mining districts in what is known as the Klondike section and they are called the Hunker and Bonanza districts. He added: "When I left Dawson City a month ago there were about 500 claims staked out and

In the two decades following the gunfight at the O.K. Corral, Wyatt wandered through the West. He spent time in Colorado, Idaho, and California before heading for Alaska in 1896 to take part in the gold rush.

FUGITIVE AND FORTUNE-HUNTER

Wyatt and Doc were next seen a month later in Silver City, New Mexico. From there they caught a train to Albuquerque. Leaving Doc Holliday behind, Wyatt and Warren Earp headed to Trinidad, Colorado, where Bat Masterson was sheriff. From there, the brothers headed to the outskirts of Gunnison, Colorado. They were sighted there, but no arrests were ever made. They

One of Wyatt and Josie's first stops after being married was Dodge City. While they were there, Wyatt cooled down a fight between Bat Masterson and his old boss, Larry Deger. During his stay, Wyatt, Bat, and several other men posed for a photograph. One wit later called it "The Dodge City Peace Commission." The photo appears on page 16 of this book.

stayed for a few months, and Wyatt made some money dealing cards.

By the end of 1882, Wyatt, Warren, and Virgil had moved to San Francisco. During this time, Wyatt began to see Josie Marcus again. In 1883, Wyatt and Josie left San Francisco together. They were eventually married.

Wyatt moved back to Gunnison. If people tried to draw him into a fight, he would defuse the situation without backing down. Wyatt was back to his old style—solving problems through intimidation, not gunplay.

From Gunnison, Wyatt and Josie traveled to Eagle City, Idaho, where Wyatt's brother James was living. The Earps staked claims on several mines, but they found no gold. However, they made money running the White Elephant saloon.

One night, a gunfight broke out, and James and Wyatt waded into the bullets. They spoke calmly, cracking jokes with both sides until everyone calmed down. Trouble followed Wyatt, but at least it wasn't his trouble.

After a few years of prospecting, Wyatt and Josie moved to San Diego. There, Wyatt's interest in gambling and horses led him to the racetrack. Eventually, he bought horses of his own. Josie gambled, too, and they lost as much money as they made.

By 1896, Wyatt and Josie had returned to San Francisco, where Wyatt was asked to referee a boxing match between Tom Sharkey and "Ruby Bob" Fitzsimmons. A crowd of 10,000 gathered at Mechanics Pavilion to see the heavyweight title bout. This was one of the first boxing matches to be fought under some new rules. Wyatt was told about several new fouls, including hitting below the belt. In the eighth round, Sharkey doubled over in pain; apparently, Ruby Bob had hit him below the belt. Wyatt declared Sharkey the winner.

The next day, Wyatt was the most hated man in San Francisco. The crowd wanted to see a knockout, not a foul. Plus, people doubted whether Sharkey was actually hit; he might have just been faking.

All the negative publicity brought Wyatt back into the spotlight. Newspaper articles were written

By 1896, Wyatt Earp had returned to San Francisco, shown as a bustling city in this late-19th-century illustration. The famous frontier lawman was asked to referee a boxing match; he didn't win any friends when he disqualified one of the fighters.

about him. Cartoons were drawn of him as a crazed, gun-toting outlaw. (In fact, Wyatt was not wearing a gun in the ring.) The violence of 15 years before had caught up to Wyatt. San Francisco was suddenly a very uncomfortable place to live.

Disgusted, Wyatt and Josie went as far away as they could—Alaska. There was a gold rush in the Yukon, and they wanted to be part of it. In Alaska, Josie and Wyatt opened the Dexter Saloon. It was very popular, and they made a lot of money. In 1901, Wyatt and Josie left Alaska with $80,000 from their saloon. They headed to Nevada to prospect for gold. Virgil and Allie joined them in 1904, but Virgil died the next year.

Two years later, Wyatt got some good news. Bat Masterson had written a detailed article about Tombstone for a magazine called *Human Life*. It was Wyatt's first good press in 25 years. The positive fame didn't pay, however, and Wyatt and Josie needed money. The profits from their saloon had been eaten up by foolish investments. Wyatt made some money by working for the Los Angeles police force. As an unofficial agent, he chased fugitives into Mexico. It was a tough job for a man in his 60s, but Wyatt was up to it.

Wyatt and Josie lived in Los Angeles for 20 years. In his last years of life, Wyatt agreed to a series of interviews with a writer named Stuart Lake. Lake's book, *Frontier Marshal*, portrayed Wyatt as a larger-than-life lawman. The nation embraced the image. Hollywood soon made him a movie hero. But the man's deeds make him difficult to pin down as simply a hero.

Wyatt died on January 13, 1929. The veteran gunfighter was defeated by the flu, without a bullet in him. As a lawman and an outlaw, Wyatt Earp had known both sides of the American West.

CHRONOLOGY

1848 Wyatt Berry Stapp Earp is born in Monmouth, Illinois, on March 19

1849 The Earp family moves to Pella, Iowa

1861 Wyatt tries to enlist in the Union Army to fight in the Civil War, but is stopped by his father

1864 The Earp family moves to California; Wyatt helps defend their wagon train

1870 Wyatt marries Urilla Sutherland in January; she dies that summer. Wyatt is elected constable of Lamar

1871 After leaving Lamar, Wyatt is arrested for stealing horses; the charges are later dropped. Hunts buffalo with Bat Masterson

1873 Disarms Ben Thompson in Ellsworth, Kansas

1874 Joins Wichita, Kansas, police force

1876 Hired as assistant city marshal of Dodge City, Kansas, where he works with Bat Masterson

1878 Wyatt meets Doc Holliday, and probably meets his common-law wife Mattie. Wyatt kills George Hoy on July 25. Silver is found in the area that would become Tombstone, Arizona

1879 The Earps arrive in Tombstone in November

1880 Curly Bill Brocius and Frank McLaury steal mules from Fort Rucker. Wyatt joins Tombstone police force

1881 Wyatt's horse is stolen by Billy Clanton. The Benson stage is held up in March; in September, the Bisbee stage is robbed. Wyatt meets Josephine Marcus. On October 26, the Earps and Doc Holliday have a gunfight with the Clantons and the McLaurys. Billy Clanton and Tom and Frank McLaury are killed; on December 28, Virgil Earp is ambushed. Two bullets hit him, crippling his arm

1882   Ike Clanton is found not guilty of the attempted murder of Virgil Earp on February 2; Morgan Earp is shot and killed while playing pool on March 18; the next day, the Vendetta Ride begins. Frank Stilwell, Florentino Cruz, Curly Bill Brocius, and possibly others are killed by Wyatt Earp, Doc Holliday, and their posse; Wyatt, Warren, and Virgil move to San Francisco, where Wyatt is reunited with Josie Marcus

1883   Wyatt returns to Dodge City. Wyatt and Josie drift from place to place, finally returning to San Francisco

1896   Wyatt referees Sharkey-Fitzsimmons fight, with unpopular results. Moves to Nome, Alaska, with Josie and opens the Dexter Saloon

1900   Warren Earp is shot and killed in Arizona

1901   Wyatt and Josie prospect for gold in Nevada; Virgil and Allie join them in 1904

1905   Virgil Earp dies. Wyatt and Josie move to Los Angeles, where Wyatt works for the police force, bringing suspects back from Mexico

1928   Stuart Lake interviews Wyatt six times for his 1931 biography, *Frontier Marshal.*

1929   Wyatt dies of the flu on January 13, 1929

GLOSSARY

alibi–proof of being somewhere else at the time of a crime.

bounty hunter–a person who tracks down outlaws in order to receive a reward.

brand–a mark put on cattle and mules with a hot iron.

brothels–houses of prostitution.

cattle drive–when a herd of cattle are moved from the range to the city where they will be transported to market.

claim–a tract of land that is staked out, especially for mining purposes.

common-law wife–a woman who is not formally married but lives with a man in a longstanding commitment.

constable–a public officer in a town or township who is responsible for keeping the peace.

enlist–to join the armed forces.

flatcar–a railroad car without sides or covering, used to carry freight.

hired gun–a man hired to fight or kill for another person.

lot jumpers–people who claim land without legal cause.

lynch–to put to death (often by hanging) through mob action without legal sanction.

marshal–an officer appointed to a particular judicial district to manage court business.

posse–a group of people summoned by a sheriff to help preserve the public peace, usually in the case of an emergency.

rustler–a cattle thief.

silver strike–the discovery of a silver vein large enough to mine.

surveyor–a person whose job it is to determine the form and extent of an area of land.

testimony–statements made under oath to be entered into a legal record, typically in court.

typhoid–a bacterial disease that causes fever, headache, and diarrhea.

vendetta–a series of violent actions taken for revenge.

wagon train–a group of settlers' wagons traveling west together.

FURTHER READING

Barra, Allen. *Inventing Wyatt Earp: His Life and Many Legends.* New York: Carroll and Graf Publishers, 1998.

Braun, Matt. *Wyatt Earp.* New York: St. Martin's Press, 1996.

Erwin, Richard E. *The Truth About Wyatt Earp.* Carpinteria, Calif.: The O.K. Press, 1992.

Faulk, Odie B. *Tombstone: Myth and Reality.* New York: Oxford University Press, 1972.

Lake, Stuart N. *Wyatt Earp: Frontier Marshal.* New York: Pocket Books, 1931.

Marks, Paula Mitchell. *And Die in the West: The Story of the O.K. Corral Gunfight.* New York: Morrow, 1989.

Parry, Richard. *The Wolf's Pack.* New York: Forge, 1998.

Tefertiller, Casey. *Wyatt Earp: The Life Behind the Legend.* New York: John Wiley and Sons, 1997.

Turner, Alford E., ed. *The Earps Talk.* College Station, Tex.: Creative Publishing Company, 1980.

Picture Credits

ROB STAEGER lives and writes near Philadelphia. A former newspaper editor, he has written many short stories for young people and several plays for older ones. This is his first book.